Afterswarm

Books by Margot Schilpp

The World's Last Night
Laws of My Nature
Civil Twilight

Afterswarm

Margot Schilpp

Carnegie Mellon University Press
Pittsburgh 2019

Acknowledgments

Deepest thanks to the editors of the following journals where
poems first appeared, often in earlier versions:

Cerise Press: "The de Havilland Comets"

The Common: "Nomenclature: Sundays" and "The Deep End"

Diode: "Meditation on the Elements: Simultaneity"

New Haven Review: "Grief"

North Dakota Review: "*Lepomis macrochirus*"

Sweet: "Poem to the Sound of an Opening Door"

Cover artwork by Mia Brownell. *Bird and Bees*, 2013. Oil on paper,
12 x 9 inches. Private collection, New York, NY.

Book design by Mariana Saric

—for Jeff—

Contents

Hover

I like to start fires, she said, lighting
the dried stalk of a green onion.
The air smelled of sandalwood and coffee,
and she could have chosen a career
to support herself, but instead
she painted bees, hives, gold hexagons
dripping with tacky honey. She painted
bees without flowers, bees stitching
time, bees that looked so real
they might zip off the canvas
into the afternoon's air. Her world
made a grammar of willing away,
of gold, of afterswarm. Sometimes,
she hid little blazes in the wings.

—One—

Poem to the Sound of an Opening Door

You can't keep culture all to yourself. You
have to share, because where would we be

without wool or commas or pepper? Some cutters
came by the walls and made windows. Look

into the strange ell of the future. See
moth wings and dragnets, the tears called down.

In Paisley, the shawls wriggle out of looms;
little tadpoles dip down the edges of hem

and fringe, draw maps back to Kashmir, Pakistan,
the mango seeds swelling in the golden sun.

What if you want to give everything back?
What if the trains' long whistles blow unending

sadnesses into the night? There is no remedy
for this yielding, no way to gather up

the peal of bells ringing across the squares.
So you must draw a conclusion: use everything

you find. Panache, gumbo, chopsticks, fins.
Wrap yourself around what's woven through.

Grab the handle and turn. Ignore the squeak
because it's night. It's day. You're here. It's now.

Seize the Day

In this large dream building she looks
for something new in the same old way.
There's a great heaviness in her chest.

It makes no sense to be afraid of change,
so she manages to move through
her days, to be in the world,

even though spirits fly into her head,
attach themselves to the roof
of her skull. They are cutouts in robes

of silver that elbow and slice.
At other times, the sunlight flashes
through the trees along the freeway,

a message, an omen: she will not
let go, won't drop the match that's struck
even as her fingers begin to burn.

She thinks of cradles, of bricks,
of how permanent a house's walls
can feel. Everything she loves

is disappearing and half
her life is gone. Her best company
is the ticking of the clock. When a puff

of smoke rises in the sky, her head
tightens with the shift from blue
to white. It is the smoke signal

telling her it's time to go, to break
the glass she is made of, to leave behind
the courtyard's ivy and her collection

of salt dips. She will never know whether—
all along—she was a shadow or the fire,
the darkness or the light.

In One Ear and Gone Tomorrow

I must've misheard, given the trash compactor
and the warming of muscles, the dozen requests
and six jays' cries. I may have thought the words

were leavened with irony or humor or plain
sadness, like the lines that make it into students' essays
or the sentences my daughters want to think

they've heard: *yes, you can stay up late, yes, eat as much
candy as your hands can grab, yes, my makeup
is your makeup.* The clear air today coupled

with bright sun and every blade of grass in the backyard
was moltenly beautiful. Every mound of leaves whispered
disturb me. All the sky's clouds arranged themselves

into shapes meant to carry someone away in a dirigible
or raft of driftwood that, in turn, would float us down
a river we'd forgotten was there. But here in Connecticut

where everyone is in a hurry and no one happens
to do anything on a whim, we're on the road. We drive
nowhere sometimes, then turn around and return.

This is a small state in a large country, a piece
of cauliflower snipped off the head, the gum
on New York's shoe. We shop at estate sales and exit

to the right. Though there's nothing telling us to stop,
every mile takes us farther away from the four walls
we huddle in every day as we tell ourselves we're fine.

Five Miles Uphill, There and Back

We bathed in the serene brutality of piano lessons
and American beer, and ate ripe bananas. The boardwalk
was thick with circus performers hiding their wedding rings

and catching a tense sunrise fluttering over the horizon.
We had thought we'd wake to tequila and baseball,
maybe even accidentally married or in a failing toy store

running out of stock, but none of the songs on our radios
had any messages for us. Words were just
words, among the ashamed and beleaguered letters

skulking off the pages into the deep of a forest.
Somehow all of the coastal birds were different hues
of blue and their feathers would have made a monk's

lifetime supply of quills. In the restaurants, storms
sank against the windows. The air: that electric suspension
of molecules waiting to bash into you if you went outside.

I went outside and followed the scent of cookies baking
outside every home on the block. No one wants cookies
with raisins, but somehow that was what there was

and we were happy, and we liked each other, and the world
turned around as we did, so we canceled out that one rotation,
and—astonished—we looked heavenward one more time

and found the color an egg shone in the grass when it fell
from the blowy nest, lost in the accident of weather, the shame
of having ruined its wings before it ever got to fly.

Dragonflies

This lamp sat in our basement
for a decade while we waited
for our girls to grow up some
and then some more, so they

wouldn't tip over the heavy
shade, make the dragonflies
fall in a shatter of metal
and glass. Around the rim,

winged, opalescent sticks
that shouldn't be able to fly
do, and the base barely holds
against the top, so you see

why we worried, with little hands
grabbing everything, grabbing
air, pulling or pushing or poking
every bit of everything we owned

before we had them, everything
we bought but hadn't looked at
in light of what might happen if,
or unless we plugged outlet covers

into every receptacle, unless
we fastened bookshelves, dressers,
televisions, and every heavy piece
of anything we worried could fall

on top of one of them if they pulled
hard enough, until one day it all
seemed unnecessary. They sit
quietly reading or doing homework,

not circling the furniture ready
to damage themselves. They have
a sense of consequences. They are
lives beginning to be without
need of any of that, or of us.

Poem for the Will

I.

To hell with classifications, the order
of things. Bring on chaos, a lack
of structure, and the innovation
we desire so that we'll buy

enough new gadgets to turn
a profit for the one lord
whose idea bounced a little
higher than the rest.

Mice may indeed make eggs
after birth. There may be hope
yet crouching in the DNA.
And you've gone

to look for the latest thing
but you instead find lack—
we've moved from wanting
more to wanting back

II.

what can't be bought:
community. The mind can be unmade
like a bed left hurriedly as the drone
of the bus grows in the distance,

toilet unflushed, breakfast uneaten, cat unfed.
It doesn't take much to convince you
that the old order's got a brand new bag:
colostomy, maybe, or Jiffy—something to write

home about that arrives without warning
and changes the days into weakness
or wisdom, a circus of change settling in.
Here there may be dragons, but how to tell?

The jackdaw knows when you're eyeing its food.
But the city looks normal enough and people
are at their stations. No haze sits
ominously over the skyline. We can relax

III.

and order another Manhattan to enjoy.
Your theories exist in trouble and all
along you'd forgotten to write them down.
Origins were lost or ascribed to someone else,

conspiracy of carelessness, bricks loosening
one by one, a rumble heard distantly
as they settle into vague patterns
that despair of the orderly use they used

to have. I'm shocked when voices come
Row, row, row your boat, gently down the stream,
because I've sung a song of sixpence. I've baked
apple pie. I've disappeared starlings

under a canopy of crust, served the King
his thrilling, moving feast. Wings clap up
across the sky. I go back to massaging the dead.
Once more a tribunal convenes: did you forget

the laws you made and made others live by?
By that point, the answer's always *yes*—
I forgot or *I didn't care.* I wanted what I wanted
enough to believe in absolutely nothing.

Nomenclature: Sundays

Sundays, my parents would pin
their names to dress clothes.
            The labelmaker's impressions formed
            letters unevenly, and at the end
of service, the tags were stuck
back into the cork. To avoid the word
                church, everyone agreed to call
                it a *fellowship*. For us, Sundays
were crafts—bunnies, pumpkins,
cornucopias—construction paper
            and glitter, Elmer's glue sticking
            everything to everything else. Blunt metal
scissors tore paper. Clothespins hung
each week's art from a piece of twine.
            The kids descended to the rooms below,
            where on other days AA meetings
and singles' teas were held.
Once we found a tiny liquor bottle
            stashed behind the john, alchemy
            of hope and failure that made
almost nothing the teacher said
real enough. There were no curtains,
                so the legs of passersby cut
                into and out of the scene. We knew
when the singing began there were six
minutes left before parents' legs
                showed through the steps' cement lattice.
                We must have hung our creations
in the cinder block halls, tape
anchoring corners and air drying
                to curls the ragged pasted flowers,
                even while above us committees
were meeting to excise references
to Jesus from hymnal and verse.
                We could have told them
                what to call things, if they'd asked—

love and honor and faith
all led us to the same names.
                 As we stretched our lengthening bones
                 against twin sheets, books beckoned
to be read. All the trees waited to be
shimmied up under the rustling leaves.

OCD

Another reflexive moment scared me
into submission, once I noticed
the calorie count on the box. Before,
I'd been scouring the sink with Clorox.
Corners on our beds had to be turned
down neatly, clothes had to be folded
precisely, the ant traps had to align
perfectly, equidistant from the baseboard
or I wouldn't be able to sleep, not if
a Q-tip poked higher than its neighbors
or the rug's fringe was tangled, or
there were water spots on the dog's bowl,
and even a wrinkle in the trash can's lining
bag could send me into a rough kind
of orbit, spinning out into the elliptical path
one degree wider each time until its course
was irrecoverably off and the world would end,
just like that. Don't think less of me. Every
time I admit my problems, I lose a friend
or two. Frankly, it's probably better
that they're gone. Grace follows a path,
and for me, that path is orderly, strict,
painful. How I got this way is impossible
to say. I was a normal kid in every way.
Just arranging my pencils from lightest
to darkest. Kids can be cruel, though.
Little differences seem big. Major deviations
from average can be met with cruelty
or fireworks. No one ever asked me
over to play, though I know now I was not
the only one. Once, in a fit of pique, I asked
Camille why her notebook was sticky,
which wasn't very nice. People these days
don't avoid me, though they know I may
rehang their coats or straighten silverware.
Quilts may be refolded. Rods may be shined.
Somewhere, in a mirror universe, the reverse
of all of this exists, and I'm flopped on a La-Z-Boy,

eating Doritos, wiping my cheesy fingers
on the arm. Toilet tissue trails from my heel
as I walk down the hall. Under the recliner,
enough pen caps and hair and dust to drive
the other me slightly mad. Victory in this place
to disorder, to leaving things piled up
on tables, to dishes in the sink and never another
stain stick, white glove, or can of Pledge.
When I imagine Paradise, though, it's a place
where evenly spaced palm trees, boulevards wide
enough to turn a car around neatly, and crisp fabric
shield us from that other place—the one where
disorder reigns. Exactly where Paradise is, I can't say,
but it's fronted, squared and waxed. Zippered slipcases rule.

Last Spring

After the hurricane, the calls came:
did you know? Did you hear

what the wind did? Have you seen the husk
of that building scattered in that field?

Sad scarecrow. Incapable and unstuffed. Sleeves
beckoning from inside the breeze. And what

of the nights or the empires lost? Or the huge oak
stretching gnarls over the hill's gentle slope,

the rain's runoff reaching the neighbor's yard
every storm? Nightly, I slid against

the shadows, closed my eyes and watched
the melodrama in reruns.

My window was a hard one to climb
from in the middle of the night.

The house returns in fragments, in dreams: slats
and nails, the loose fireplace stone, the broken

gas jet. A decade on: the precise shape
of a dislodged piece of tape hanging between

Thermopane, the sink's fond chip.
It is not rare, this human desire to collect

the past in stills laid out in grids. Across
the street, the neighbors' camper parked

for weeks. A cardinal made her nest in chrome.
Hope traveled downhill like water.

Night

Eleven already, and I'm scuttling the plan to stay up. I lay waste
to the hospital corners and relax, already, relax, because the moon

is afraid of its shadow, of its green cheese and jalapenos and every
row of corn stands shining in the moonlight, rows of weapons ready

to fire at will, ready to go staticky and thistly with the summer's heat.
The glow of light that threatens to reveal who was where and what

was what blinks a little in the atmosphere. It strobes a bit on July's
dance floor, and it takes a day or two to launder the sweatshirts and

cutoffs we wear in the yellow field. See them hanging on the clothesline
frittering away time and the instruments to measure it by. No pins

can fasten our hopelessness to the line. No basket can contain all
the loads of fear we're harvesting from the earth's reluctance

to cooperate with our one and only plan: use up what's here
and keep no tally. In the darkness we can pretend we don't see

anything at all. We don't notice the faint hash marks stubbling
cement and wood. We can't see the blood pooling around the halo

of wavy hair. But a red-headed woodpecker clasps the bark
and bobs against the tree. Shouldn't we be reassured by something

natural and familiar, something soothing that keeps a beat,
something that carries us into the silt left behind after the rains?

Lepomis macrochirus

—for Paula

I slip the comb through your hair,
separate it into three ropes I'll weave,
marry. You've grown out your bangs so you can hide
more easily behind long strands. And suddenly: bluegill.
I am thinking of bluegill, how they fight the line.

Then: I should clean out all our closets, make room
for golf clubs or drain cleaner, but in our home
the feminine outnumbers three to one. One more,
if you count the cat, which we do, and women collect
clothes and bottles of shampoo, and they love sandals

and lord knows what else (well, I know what else)—
like some compulsive lover navigating between
years-old stacks of newspapers in narrow halls.
There's time to shop, but less time to cull.
Your hair glistens with each turn of my wrists.

The green flash below the water twists.
The cat sleeps on, so the foot of my bed
is cluttered, too. Forgive me for the sixty shirts
that crowd the closet rod, the shoes that don't get
put away. To understand clutter, you have

to experience its lack. There must have been days
when whole squadrons of geese returned
and days when the crocuses were opening
their blooms to the street. Anyone driving by
would have seen minuscule bursts of deep purple

stars. Blurring the line between out there and in here
is important, because anyone walking
by would have seen the green jackets draped over
the tulip's shoulders. The sunsets here
have been full of bees. In the distance, I hear

fireworks or guns, the friendship of sound
with breaking, with every subtle end

of every bad movie. I watch your single flame
grow into branches of fire, a burning canopy
of regret that dampens each future day.

There were whole days when I forgot
to check the cat's food and I would hide out
waiting for something. You came to me
with blood and your character swept past, unformed,
brittle. No one showed me how to hold

the bottle, how to pull your tiny arm through
a narrow sleeve. I learned to place my hand
across your chest so you slept and the days
were blur and grind, and then the days were one
similar moment taking the place of the one just past.

There were great stirrings of noise that came
from your throat. I would cower and cave
to the clear need as I genuflected beside your crib.
All the angels I'd ever heard of arrived when you did:
they are here now, hovering, silent creatures

that skim by us. They are green shadows.
Your braid swims down the center of your back
and I fasten the tail with a sparkling band.
The bluegill have no messy plot, no cruel
passivities: the core is obvious and dreams chug

into the station right on time. I see the repetitions
and reminders signaling when the trapdoor opens
to swallow the light. No step is too light to trigger it,
no phantasm opens up the brilliant swallowtails
and candied apples that offer themselves

in black and white. But I can make this anything
I like, and it will stand. The stars in their teacups
wink at me through their quilts and hems.

Or the fish—let's send him out for food.
He's hunting down some kind of meal to take away

the gnawing in his little fish stomach. He's O-ing
his fishy bluegill mouth and sucking in food
and spitting out excess water, and he's happy
in his bluegill world. And on some days he sweeps
across his pond, meanders through some warmer

spots and colder patches where he rests,
for a moment, touches his fishy mouth to a slick
rock in case there's food. Say he's still hungry
and still on patrol, and he makes his way across
the waters gathering fish along the way. But I digress

because I must. I can't remember the parts
of a fish, the labels that apply to fish—the habitats,
breeding patterns—and I'm afraid because this happens
with more than a simple stupid bluegill—whole
continents of words I can't recall, though I can trap

them here: sequin, busybody, usurp, canine, lapdog,
marchesa, hula hoop, rung, tower, mundanity, loss.
I believe the signs when they advise not to enter.
Not to turn. I believe in the sudden change of plans.
How could I not? So often I search for the perfect word,

the one that will finally allow me to confirm at last
what I've suspected for years: I'm changing
into a wordless, thoughtless imbecile who soon will
not remember her own name. I return to the bluegill,
whom I've named Happy, the easiest word

on the planet since it's somewhat like a verb,
and also like some simple destination, like making
your hair into the braid that holds everything
together—the long line of memories, the future,
and the beauty you'll see and have no words for.

A Translation

They say that people who have children
can't make great art. That may be true,
and it may be that the world's a desolate road

filled with widening potholes. But I am casting
under the cold stars for the line I promised
you I'd write. Nowhere are the doves pressing

their breasts against the stone these days,
and everywhere I see graffiti and tattoos,
ink and paint splashing the skin, the cinder

block, the undated melodrama announcing
another difficult evening not spent at home.
I seem to think in threes: my three loves

who buffer the stillness and pierce me
with their triumvirate. We are in quarters,
each in her own bed, each with her own brush,

a scowl or giggle crossing each face, and each
day a lot to learn. I am consumed by not knowing
the future, and I do not remember the past.

What did I do before? I think I must have been
smarter and lonelier and certainly less
amused. I almost never found myself on the floor.

The days sawed across the clock, leaving
a trail of sawdust and an echoing tick. Forgive
me when I say that I was no one, before.

I was someone, yes. But not someone
worth thinking about for too long, when
instead you could count the stars and their invisible

tendons gripping us, pulling our eyes upward
against a backdrop of barren darkness,
a bucket of rippling water reflecting the ancient sky.

Untitled Poem to My Daughters, Attempt #39

I thought I never wanted children, and maybe I was afraid
of that neighborhood with its burns and abandonments,

its aerial views of pets' graves and swing sets forlorn
against a fish-scale fence. The view from here is warmer,

full of soft night breathing and painted figures drying
paper to curls. That other life might have been fine.

That other life might have grafted words with silences
casting shadows in tidy rooms. There, I would have found

quietness that stiffens the back, stillness that hums beyond
the body's margins. What else could have telegraphed

the skin's dilemmas? My cells recalled who was in charge,
and meant to change before they ever did. The ending I chose,

I chose to thwart a foregone conclusion. Every night,
terrors ended as the light was switched on, and the silk

of certainty slipped down my shoulders as I straightened
and faced the door. My hands reached out for the glass knob

and my summer face found the anchors it needed to mount itself.
No one can say truly how the future will arrive, but I have two

girls who awaken each morning, ready to believe whatever
I teach them is true, and I take seriously the solemn job of love.

Visitation at the Automat

I knew the lice and the macaw, saw the fields
overrun with seeds that would never grow.
This was the busiest season: ethics and popcorn,
both exploding. I wonder. A group of children,
rocking. Thank you for folding everything I love
into one small box, but I fear my teeth falling out.

I fear fire and deportation. I went into the dark lake
with everyone I knew: we watched boxing
where the ropes held us all out of the ring.
There were no longer any punches I couldn't pull.
I handled my headphones and airplane security
with ease. I found the lights of the paparazzi avoided

me. The horizon called *here*. Come into the distance
and let go of the left hook you wanted to throw.
If it isn't Tijuana, it's Boise, or Fargo or Des Moines.
If it isn't boxing, it's golf or Pilates. A grand act:
a bow and a bit of grain into the trunk of a tree.
If my lip's swollen, look at the other fighter's knuckles.

See how the indentation of his ring is reversed
in the pillow of my skin? See the revolution of love,
the change in outright ownership? You do, you don't,
he she they may. A blank look may mean you're thinking
of a lie, but if all of this is being scored,
let me not have points deducted for screaming.

Mastery of Smoky Shadows

—for Leah

Sometimes you can see them, shifting against the wind,
winding across the field under the fence slats, brown,
gray, terrible, tenacious, holding on to the last of the light,

or slipping under the haunches of a Guernsey cow.
Feel their unwillingness to move into the realm
of happiness. They want a reign of unspeakable dolor,

a sad ending to a sad story. They cling and cower.
They will not be put off by sunny hayrides or a job
well done. And often they seem to billow behind

the insubstantial trees, or spread out like patches
of spring violets bound by a rock here or a post there,
their insistence on blur and tease rippling the whole

spectrum. The eyes diagnose and then darken, and suddenly
a field of sunflowers springs its yellow surprise. This is not
what you came to see, this shining archipelago, this golden

communion. You stole the last of the light and turned it
into time. But no one asked for the unconditional. No one
told the old stories again or understood how the paucity

of objects limited the view. There were multiples,
redundancies, movements on a loop that played over
and over. None of the stories we hear are true. Not one

of the tree trunks or barns or gates wants to give up
dimension for substance, and all our tortured
wishing makes nothing happen, everywhere, again.

—*Two*—

Transit Authority

History tests the bus against us
to make sure the people swelling
into the doors aren't old coconuts
or stucco, or slang for *hipster*, but
a neck and body, a $10 bill banded
to the ankle of a little boy.

Rosalie remembers her bus rides and rolling
heaves over the rails as something
like access: an addition between Sixth
and Broadway where the darkness
bore a breeze, and news exposed cards
sent each year to the newly voted.

The plot thickens. Kathy works from home,
and finds a lot of votes she hadn't counted.
A lot is just enough for a win, which
may be like a necklace of candy worn
to the office party, so many are gobbling
at the folds of her throat.

Thomas must have looked up each night
at so many stars, he felt the backs
of their scales rustling against his legs
as he stoked the fire. There were pines
and sheep, a screen door banging against
the cedar shake. He calls down the squad

of logs to roll. He rings a bell for supper, unaware.
May I sing shallow in the garden.
May I transcribe cabins and porches and sunsets
and yellow Blue Birds in the streets.
May history's plumage unruffle
as we call it home to roost.

Meditation on the Elements: Simultaneity

> *These days are a great blessing to men on earth; but the*
> *rest are changeable, luckless, and bring nothing. Every-*
> *one praises a different day but few know their nature.*
> –Hesiod, *Works and Days*

<Au>

Don't ask *how the gods and mortal men sprang*
from one source, because there are school buses
and lemon sharks and bananas, all gold enough
to blind you. You walk through a field of daffodils
on that cool day that feels warm after months
of ice, of thick mittens and hats that muffle sound.
With all the layers, we refuse to yield. No sign
is bright enough to warn: something's crossing
against the amber light, and let it be cowardice,
or a reign of bees, or the feel of fresh butter
in your mouth. Turn back: *And they lived like gods*
without sorrow of heart, remote and free from toil
and grief, if that's possible, though it must be.
Somewhere. Not here. Here's a marigold flaming
from the ground like a rivet. Here's a reflection
of the sun magnified in an ordinary puddle,
the kind a kid jumps across wearing a slicker
and boots after a quick storm. Here's an omelet
sputtering on the stove, and ears of corn pushing
against the wind. Across the street, a hearse idles.
The mourners glance down to check their watches.
If only things were simple. *When they died,*
it was as though they were overcome with sleep,
and they had all good things; for the fruitful earth
unforced bare them fruit abundantly and without stint.
Simplicity's for angels and dogs, not some schmuck
running for a taxi, cheese sandwich spoiling
in his briefcase. Not much is easy and even less
makes sense. We can't explain our system of error
and compromise. We know what turns the skin
gold and we can fix flats and prices, then sell high,

<Ag>

though it's *less noble by far. It was like the golden race*
neither in body nor in spirit. A child was brought up
at his good mother's side an hundred years, an utter
simpleton, playing childishly with Botox, latex,
the substances of pleasure bought on credit. Many
pregnant mares urinated to soften the effects
of time. We can replace other kinds of plumbing
with plastics, shiny chrome fixtures that turn
on a dime, and on the bulletin board signs appear:
Lost Keys! Lost Cat! Lost youth is not so far
behind, when the brain tells you there are ways
to ease from behind the wheel of a trip no one wants
to take. You could arrive to find a friend
in his own home. But when they were full grown
and were come to the full measure of their prime,
they lived only a little time in sorrow because of their
foolishness, unless the story's end is its beginning,
a commencement attended by dolphins and whales,
things with tails and fins, sleek gray shapes
whittling through time against a backdrop of tongues.
There's not enough time in the world to make up
for what's been missed, but we try and try: *for*
they could not keep from sinning and from wronging
one another, nor would they serve the immortals, nor
sacrifice on the holy altars of the blessed ones
as it is right for men to do wherever they dwell,
unless they dwell too long on surfaces, the glittery
locket holding a hank of drying hair. The proof
of faith is a dainty chain tethering what's most
precious to the wattle of her neck. Turn back: the sky

<Cu+Sn>

blushed toward the hour, and it *was terrible and strong.*
They loved the lamentable works of Ares and deeds
of violence; they ate no bread, but were hard of heart,
unlike the doughy peacocks prancing in Brioni
and Kiton. If all this sounds terribly sad, it is,
but not because the shells fell to the earth, dulling
the sense of time or space, and not because there hung
in many homes a brown haze that obscured the sun
so the shine on weapons dimmed. They took up arms
against themselves. They misinterpreted sculpture,
the way a criminal tries to guess what answer
may suit best, or makes him look less like himself.
Great was their strength and unconquerable the arms
which grew from their shoulders on their strong limbs.
Their armour was of bronze, and their houses of bronze,
and of bronze were their implements: there was no
black iron, unless you count droplets of blood that
dried into the dirt. A favorite pastime, that.
We loved to count, and taught others to count, too:
one, two, buckle my shoe, three, four, shut the door,
but already the vapors had slipped across the rings
where the matador challenged the bull. Go back:
grim war and dread battle destroyed a part of them,

<Fx>

but to the others father Zeus the son of Cronos gave a
living and an abode apart from men, and made them dwell
at the ends of earth. And they live untouched except
for the internet, which zigged across the planet as
nothing ever had before. The possibilities invade
every cell of every hero—appear here and there at once,
save everything you can, and more, because not only
can you be in many places at once, you are more you
than ever before. Your reputation precedes you
and it follows you, and you follow all your hero friends
on Twitter. You friend other heroes' friends and so on,
and so on, until you reach a certain limit and the
game warden has to pull you aside and remind you
what is meant *by sorrow in the islands*
of the blessed along the shore of deep swirling Ocean,
happy heroes for whom the grain-giving earth
bears honey-sweet fruit flourishing thrice a year, far
from the deathless gods and their potted biographies.
Sure, everyone will suspect you are not the child
of your father, and everyone will try to spirit you away
with candied plums and secret missives smuggled
into the palace of your life. Everyone will suppose
your death was not as mundane as it seemed—crash
of metal, crash of rhinos, crash-landing landing
you in some mysterious swamp no one knows
the name of. You are not here now, and no one

<Fe>

succeeds you. *For now truly is a race of iron, and men*
never rest from labour and sorrow by day,
and from perishing by night; and the gods shall lay
sore trouble upon them, in the form of technical glitches
that send a whole city into darkness at noon, the bit
of idle time chomped and spat to the ground.
If we can't load this page or that, we die or think
we will—the speed of quitting's picking up.
Go back again: discover *there will be no favour*
for the man who keeps his oath or for the just
or for the good; but rather men will praise
the evil-doer and his violent dealing. Much like
faux news or the town gossip's shriveled tongue
curling around the old lies: if only things were
simple again. The world twists on its axis,
a figure skater tightening her scratch spin
who wants nothing but to go faster without losing
the details we enjoy. Go forth and season
your skillets with reason and peace, the myths
brought down, when *strength will be right*
and reverence will cease to be; and the wicked
will hurt the worthy man, speaking false
words against him, and will swear an oath upon them.
Oh, maybe that was all right when there were matters
that mattered, but now, it's all the same to everyone
who can buy portable media storage, spin
a drive to protect the data and make backups.
Let's secrete them here, there, everywhere,
in the resurrection plants and in the water bear.
We can return to them when it's time, but not
now, when *bitter sorrows will be left for mortal men,*
and there will be no help against evil. I'm ironing
the last of the shirts from the basement, trying to
de-crease the fabric so that it hangs smooth.
Everything that's happened can happen again.
We still refuse to yield. At the edge of our vision:
the gates across the street, swung open to admit faith.

44

Arts and Crafts on Venus

Her hand clips the wire, then ties the filament against
the wingspan of her neck. She practices

awakening. She practices denying herself
nothing. And there is nothing

to forget now, with all the wind standing still
and the American plains of her barren phone book.

Some say glue for the crumbling spines of books.
Some say red leather bindings and mascara

the color of old blood. I say watch the window,
the window, the window: escape

the sunlight's burning prayer
that ruins a perfect afternoon. Across the room,

the radiator breathes and rattles, and a small hiss
escapes her lips. The smallest movements

of the mouth can't seal the positions
of the stars, but they can purse the horizon

into dormancy, into a pinstruck moonstream,
into black anchors leaking frail protest

at every tug, every accidental drop
and smear, and all the galaxy's regrets.

Decorah, Iowa: Night and Day on the Nest

look about the same: an eagle preening
or an eagle feeding her three new hatchlings,

each a fuzzy gray wobble. They sleep a lot,
but every hour or two, three beaks point

skyward when food arrives. The three chicks
are nudged centerward for naps. So what is it

that makes this show so watchable, since
we could be tuning in to *Criminal Minds*

or *Law and Order*, or any number of mindless
dramas? Maybe it's their nest: five feet

across, it weighs half a ton. Maybe
it's the unlikelihood of its survival,

perched as it is eighty feet off the ground
near a fish hatchery. Maybe it's the sound

of the wind and the birdsong that reminds me
I haven't heard the haphazard calls of birds

in the morning since we installed new windows
that muffle the outdoors. The camera pans

and zooms, stays on day and night for people
to drop in and watch the birds as they hunch

into the nest against the wind. When it rains
their dazzling, bloody larder shines.

The de Havilland Comets

All through those last flights the cracks spread
like tiny silver zippers. People sat strapped
to the seats and looked out the square windows

across the earth's sweep. Flights took off.
Flights landed. Flights flew from London
to Rome, from Berlin to Cairo. Shatner's goon

on the airplane's wing is fearsome, but imagine
being a passenger on the de Havilland Comet,
looking out the window at the distant cotton clouds

and smoking a Dunhill while mulling the wine list.
I'm bending a paper clip back and forth,
feeling it get warm, and watching the crook

lighten and twist. If ever we wanted engineers
to re-test something thoroughly, it would be
planes, and they thought they had. Hours

of pressurization, shields between the engines
and fuel tanks, reinforced fuel lines, new
smoke detectors. None of it mattered

because no one knew the Comets had exploded
after fractures from rivets started the planes'
skin peeling away as the metal fatigued.

I can't smooth the paper clip to its pristine
sleekness, and can't forget the Comets. I push
on them just to the point of breakage. Beyond.

A Version

Remember the days in the other house:
it was like love
in a different flavor.

Savor the age of insects or the plant when
it was foolishly
in flower. Nostalgia

does not examine your desires. We are
accustomed to the anthems,
to the new platforms.

The wood is all there is to consume. Affirm
the yellowed notes,
the dirty scribbles

where she is seated: her hands rest on her knees,
and she carries the small
provisions. A little gatherer

is following. It supervises in a certain harmful
manner. It is the glance that proves
why one decade

from now is the mysterious solo. I admit that I am
cheering for the interior. Maybe people will
comment on a version

of ego which could one day turn over. The table still
evokes a sharp desire to remain upright:
a platform is an admirable thing.

Leaving a Marriage

<Attending a Play>
In the dark, between acts and alone, I decided my marriage
was over. Checklists budded on the branches of the leaving
tree: find an apartment . tell him . call mother . divide the
music, towels, dishes, dressers, coins . change address .
renew friendships . begin some other journey . enjoy . work
. travel . feel

<Packing Boxes>
The chicken boxes were the best, waxed and handled, stiff
cardboard that could hold up to anger. Even driving to find
boxes was therapeutic. I learned when and where stores
discarded them, and filled my car with boxes that held the
shape of emptiness. Other boxes smelled of feet or food that
had leaked, the cardboard slightly soggy and separating.

<Flowers in Bloom>
On each trip to the car, I saw azaleas. Dark leaves waved
so long, come back again soon. The trip became routine: six
steps, a bit of sidewalk, two more steps, and inside the door
to pick up another waiting box for the balancing against
stomach and hip before reversing the process. The fuchsia
blooms said *stop*, while their green leaves shouted *go. Go.*

<A Hotel Stay>
Each night at the hotel was a palindrome of almost-grief.
Their clean linens sent me back to eras where I did not
belong and did not want to go. Every night, as I lay down
and clicked through channels, the sheets absorbed sweat
and sadness. I had arrived less than a block from where
I'd started, but it was another country. It was mine. It was
mine, and I wanted to find its name.

Courage

All the words I don't know terrify me.
What if I die before I learn the one
I'll need to describe my feelings for you?
When I see photographs from your prom,
there's a pretty girl beside you
and I mark that she's dark-haired, thin,
as young as we all were then. Why are we
our most beautiful selves when we are empty
inside? We are victims. Hosts.
Like hierophants, we age to show how
it's going to be done. We suffer the sagging
skin, though it does not make us sages.
Only experience does that. Time's arrow shot
through flesh carries the sadness of gravity.

The Deep End

I still hadn't learned to swim, after the MacVicar's pool,
and this pool's water was cold enough to mask
the pain from knees banged and knuckles scraped

across the gritty paint. The sun boiled all our secrets out,
left us empty and tired, but each day our parents dropped us
at the Ramada Inn pool's door, then drove away

to grocery shop or do whatever parents must
when they disappear from view. I entered the water
only so I could say I had, but the fountain of fear

rose and stayed—like a stubborn knot, like a snake,
like a bite of something spoiled noticed too late—
It is years before I learn I can turn it off for a while

by joking or paddling, but not by huddling
in the dressing room with my friend as we sneak
glances at the bodies we pray we'll have in two years

or at those we hope we won't in thirty. And not
by a hard crush on my friend's older brother.
When I think of pure fear, I am entering the water

at the smooth lip of that hotel's pool. Or I am slipping below
the surface of that other water, earlier. I have to work
to reconstruct the cautions to walk, the bright beach

towels draped over sticky chairs, the heat of the sauna
and the hissing stones from which drying steam rose.
Every day, the family cars will drive up, honk,

and almost in one motion we will shoot upward
against the water's force, half-turn to perch
on the pool's edge, rise, and gather everything.

Still dripping, we will vanish under the humid sun.
But with no effort at all comes what came just before:
a stunning whiteness that reflects off the concrete, passes

through the glass sliders, and makes shimmers of light
where we pull ourselves under the water to sit cross-legged
on the pool's deep floor. I am petrified, but we hold hands,

the three of us in a tight circle. We open our eyes and blink
as the bubbles powering out of our noses keep us
anchored in the time when, briefly, we can live without air.

My Version of Physics

Asked for the key to the loft,
then turned into stone and tears,
a lattice of pain that grew
from a map of the shore.

The past devoured the past.
The inky recollection colored
us like soup. We pinned copper
wire along doorways and decks.

Simple, you said. And it was.
Unless not. Unless the rough
molar your tongue returned to
all night crumbled into the cave

of your mouth. Words mattered
and didn't. It's wrong to betray
the tribe—to be fat with grief
at the end of a parade, all

cacophony and swagger,
the past made whole, and
your fond sleepwalking toward
all those kindred molecules.

Elegy for a Former Self Who Misunderstood the Nature of Time, Space, and Everything Else

I resembled a wobbly cart,
an iffy wire, a bronze statue broken
at the elbow or knee or neck, a fault

line running against the horizon
while the scenery behind me changed.
First, it had been a violet sunrise turning

to ocher, then daylight took over, but then,
a glade filled with ripe peach trees.
Then a burned-out cityscape, a black llama,

a fire. I could not recall arriving, nor
could I leave, yet the ones at the tables, calling
for another round of ouzo, let me stay,

and stay I did, until the sunrise pulled
the shade of the sky down. Then I rested
and wondered again what made the sky

show us coronas or asteroids, what made blue
blue, what word I had forgotten to write
down so it was forever lost in the tides

of memory. I came up with answers, not one
of which was right, but each of which satisfied.
I spent the night lonely or broken or left

in the shadow of the rains that came,
blustering against the panes and streaking
the view of outside so that all things looked

almost the same and nothing was visible
as itself. Everything blended into a smeared
wetness and somehow that made me happy—

to know that nothing anywhere was
what it was from that one vantage point
at that one point in time: everything

could have been anything, anything
could have been nothing, nothing
could have been nothing else, and I was

seeing it all, for the first and only time,
for the last and only time, then and
then, and never again, forever. Amen.

Grief

In the kitchen, the heads of lettuce are lonely.
They wait
in the dark for your hands to press against their ears.

The corn unzips
its silk, a striptease with tassels just for you.
You never use

the seasoned iron skillet that came from your mother,
never twist
the stove's knobs anymore. In your kitchen, flames

are only ghosts
of flames, cold shapes shivering in echo or pantomime.
Against the drain,

the sink's sponge is a hard, green oblong, and
a residue
of bubbles climbs the stainless steel. In your kitchen,

no one spreads
out dough with the rolling pin, no one drops cookies
on a sheet.

No measuring spoons rattle. All the spices stay
in their own
quaint jars, quiet and sealed. The teakettle's whistle is

a memory
ramping up in the humid air. In your kitchen the potholders
and placemats

and aprons and dishrags sit limp. The dip tray stays
in the cupboard.
The cutting board could just as well have stayed a tree.

Pygmalion Effect

I rest in the flush of a sunset.
There aren't words on the tongue
that fasten humanity's shawl

tighter than *thank you,* but the light
turns itself down and down
and teaches me to swear.

On the rocks below: several
thousand graves. Or, not graves
but the outlines of people

who've rustled through here.
Recalibrate the dusk, for I've fallen
into disrepair and when it's not

quite dark I look my best.
That's when we'll meet.
Hour of lavender. Hour of blur.

Pay no attention to the voices
warning of pestilence, famine.
Only the crying is real. Far away

seems farther away than before,
when trees arced over marble
and a fence was fastened to the field.

Delicate leaves and hardier shadows
trembled. Everything
is the only shape it will ever be.

Transplant

A misbehaving heart transplant recipient
dies in a wreck as he's being chased
by the cops, and isn't it a shame

that the scarce heart could have beaten
for years longer in the chest of a banker
or the rib cage of a vet making decisions

about animals' lives day after day?
Who knows what awful crimes
are committed in melancholy, in

the name of someone else, in anguish
or happiness, in the blood-rivers
of war or poverty's dust? No one

had to tell the boy with someone else's heart
to run: he'd been trying to outpace
the future he stole for going on two years.

And maybe that's how we reconcile the story.
We assign blame. We make someone the villain.
We give something away and wish we had it back.

Omega

After the tongues stopped
flitting across the sky's arc
but before gravity allowed everything
        not tethered to fall to earth—
coniferous trees, dogs unchained,
every blooming cactus
growing in every desert—
        the end began. Clearly,
this was big. Definitely, this was something
you couldn't avoid noticing.
Each to her own bed. Fine quilts
        cover the resting body,
the dying bodies. Geriatric
women fingering the borders
they'd pieced, threads familiar
        and precise. However their bodies
lay was how they would be found
in a hundred or a thousand years.
If you pray, this would be a good time.
        Just in case. Knowledge slid
down the candles and settled into pools
of cooling wax. Lore
replaced science. Maybe we were happy
        then or could be.
Next to belief, what did we have but feelings?
Only the frilled duvets
and dried powders told the story
        we could not. Providing a way
into the future became our only map.
Quaint lavender nosegays
and gingham tablecloths appeared in all
        the shops. Relying on history
got us nowhere. So we sang. Truly
magnificent notes moved
in our airwaves, a choir of crepey throats
        warbling half-recalled tunes.

Under the faint blue sky, it became all right
to imagine tears.
Vowels stretched across the ears' canvases.
        When one tone ended, another
took its place, and so on. Exactly no one
refused to sing. Yet the music stopped,
all at once. Silence took its place. Zinnias
        grew from the earth's green notes.

40°30'07"N 114°01'56"W

Kamikaze mosquitos blanket the water—
they're thick in the weird humidity.
This is the desert, and mostly it's dry.

But around Blue Lake for ten or twelve feet
there's a swampy zone where they must lay eggs
and wait and find themselves drawn to the heat.

On the way here, dust trailed from the car's tires
as we made our way down the road. I call it a road,
but it was more like dirt ruts through scrub grasses,

driven often enough to tamp down new growth.
Blue Lake is a geothermal pond.
The cars here have scuba decals. If you wanted

to find a place as far from anywhere as possible,
this might be it. It takes an hour to drive six miles
into nowhere. Everywhere on the horizon is empty

land, salty air, haze. As night falls, it seems every star
in every galaxy winks on. Divers say the lake has art
inside: sculptures of an ant, a scorpion, a shark.

A headless woman pushing a lawnmower.
But we don't see any of that. The surface
is where we stay and it's where we must belong.

The depths are not meant for us. We sit
in our camp chairs, have a drink, and watch
the ancient stars to chart our course to nowhere.

Till It's Gone

There was so much travel, I sickened
of scenery. I longed for a view
        I could count on to be two
        days the same. In my head,
a reel clicks and shows me still
moments lost. I wear

        a nubby pale pink coat. I miss
        my Siamese cat. The crank
of my bedroom window sticks
then comes loose all at once.
        One stone in our fireplace wiggles,
        a little like a loose tooth. I spend

weeks pretending I can't walk,
and must prance down our teak hall
        to move from room to room.
        Time seemed not to pass at all.
Yet here is the everyday everything,
the plans for meals and the morning's

        rush. There are appointments, classes
        to meet, grading and planning, making
sure everyone is where she belongs
each day. But there are shimmers: the roof
        of a chalet in Innsbruck, geraniums
        blooming in the balcony window planters.

A plate of salami, some dry brown bread,
and an egg standing in a cup. Embroidered
        napkins folded and waiting. Now, the world
        burns and grows, beauty syncopated
against loss, and I let in only shards.
Was that or is this the world I love?

Afterswarm

Before I wake up, there's a twisted wind
      in the fields. Pot roasts prance and dancing
  girls bum cigarettes in the movie theater
lobby. The rushing wind goes on. Half
   a wafer and half a bottle of wine makes
for a pretty awful night, one with gurgling
      and helpfulness alternating their turns to drive.
In some of the scenes of this film, time
     is skipped. Scenes flash by so fast
  they're scarcely noticeable, and isn't everything
like that? We don't notice what's wrong
     until the big hole swallows the Corvettes
or the hundred cars pile up and block
  the highway for hours. One trillion sets of eyes
and vapor trails across the night sky.
                        Your beloved
     country turned strange and dangerous, a shell
of itself and siccing itself on you like a rabid dog
  you can't bear to put down. Your family gone.
Your friends across vast nets of molecules
  impossible to cross. Your interior: a ball of wax,
a broken marble. Crystallized honey. You fetch

the daily things. You go on. There's nothing else to do.